THE COMPLETE APA 7th EDITION GUIDE

The Easiest Book for Proper Formatting, Writing, and Citations to Create the Perfect Research Paper or Academic Document

GREGORY DIXON

Contents

PREFACE

Welcome to The Complete APA 7th Edition Guide, the easiest book on how to format, write, and cite correctly so you can make the best research paper or academic document. This book will teach you everything you need to know about APA style, with a focus on the changes made in the 7th version.

The American Psychological Association created APA style, which is used a lot in the social sciences, education, and other academic fields. It gives you rules and instructions on how to format, cite, and show scholarly work. Since the 7th version came out, there have been big changes to the rules for formatting, citing sources, and writing in general.

If you want to show your work professionally and ensure its credibility, whether you are a student, researcher, or academic, you need to know how to use APA style. It is the goal of this book to give you a complete and easy-to-use guide that makes it easier to understand and follow APA 7th edition rules.

Part I, "Understanding APA 7th Edition," tells you what you need to know to start reading this book. You will learn about APA style, be told about the changes made to the most recent version, and be reminded of how important it is to format, write, and cite properly in academic papers.

Here in Part II: Formatting Guidelines, we go over the details of how to format your paper in APA style. This section goes over all the important parts of formatting, like how to make a title page, style headings and subheadings, and use lists, tables, and figures correctly.

It looks at the rules and customs for mentioning sources inside the text of your paper in Part III: In-Text Citations. It gives clear instructions on how to use the author-date format to cite sources, with different examples for group writers and secondary sources.

On top of the rules for citing sources in the text, Part IV: Reference List is all about making a complete and correct list of references. It tells you how to properly format your references so they follow the rules of APA style and properly cite different types of sources, like books, journal articles, websites, reports, and government papers.

Part V: Writing Guidelines looks more closely at the parts of APA style that have to do with writing. This part has very helpful tips for making your writing better. These tips cover everything from making your writing clearer and shorter to mastering grammar, punctuation, capitalization, and bias-free language.

In Part VI: Special Situations, we talk about problems that experts often face. This part talks about how to organize research papers and how the different parts should be put together. It also talks about the specific needs for writing theses and dissertations and gives instructions on how to submit and publish manuscripts.

To help you even more, we've added an appendix with sample papers that show how to follow the rules in the APA 7th version correctly. A glossary and index are also at the end of the book to make it easier to find what you're looking for.

The Complete APA 7th Edition Guide is the best book for anyone who wants to learn how to write in APA style, whether they are a beginner looking for a step-by-step guide or an expert writer wanting to know more about the latest rules.

Join us as we learn the ins and outs of APA style. This will give you the tools you need to write perfect academic papers and set you up for success in study and school.

1

What is APA Format

To fully understand APA style, it is important to first know where it came from, what it's meant to do, and what it means in the world of academic writing. As an introduction, this chapter tells you everything you need to know about APA style and its main parts.

1.1 Where APA Style Came From

A group of psychologists and business managers got together in 1929 to make a set of rules for science writing. This is where APA style got its start. The American Psychological Association, with the help of a group of experts led by Edwin B. Newman, wanted to make a standard format that would make academic work in the social sciences more clear, consistent, and trustworthy.

1.2 What APA Style Is Trying to Do

APA style is based on the idea that writers should be able to clearly and briefly explain their research and ideas. By following the rules of APA style, writers can make sure that people all over the world can access and understand their work. APA style also encourages accuracy, trustworthiness, and professionalism in school writing.

1.3 Parts of the APA Style

There are many parts to APA style that work together to make the structure and presentation of a paper. Some of these elements are rules for layout, rules for citing sources, and rules for writing style and language use. Each part is important for getting information across correctly and properly.

1.4 When APA Style Is Used

The APA style came from the area of psychology, but it is now used in many other fields as well. Many areas in the social sciences, like education, sociology, anthropology, and communication studies, now use this style instead of others. Also, professionals in many areas, like business, nursing, and public health, use APA style for their academic writing all the time.

1.5 Why using APA style is a good idea

When writing for school, using APA style has a number of benefits. For starters, it makes sure that all research papers are the same, which makes it easier for readers to understand and find their way around the content. Second, APA style encourages honesty and correctness by giving you a standard way to list and cite sources. Also, knowing how to use APA style is very important in the business and academic worlds because it shows that the writer is a credible researcher or teacher.

1.6 Changes in the 7th Edition and the History of APA Style

Like any other style guide, APA changes over time to reflect new academic goals and ways of doing things. With the release of the 7th version, there were major changes made to make formatting, referencing, and writing easier to understand. We'll be talking about the changes made by the 7th version throughout this book so that you can get the most up-to-date tips and tricks.

If you look into the basic ideas talked about in this chapter, you will have a good idea of where APA style came from, what its goals are, and how it can be used. The next parts will go into more detail about formatting, citations, and writing rules, but this information will help you get started. Let's start this APA style journey to find out how to write scholarly work that meets the best standards of quality and professionalism.

Formatting Guidelines

We learned about the history and goals of APA style in Chapter 1, which helped us understand how important it is for academic writing. Now, let's look more closely at the rules for structure that APA style sets out. These rules cover a lot of different parts of document style, like title pages, headings, margins, page numbers, and more.

2.1 The Title Page

The title page is the first page of your document and tells you what you need to know about the paper. It usually has your name, the title of your paper, the name of the school where you work, and sometimes an author note. The title should be short and clear, and it should accurately describe what your study is about.

2.2 Titles

Using headings in your paper makes it easier to read and understand. In APA style, there are five levels of titles, and each one shows a different level of importance. Headings at Level 1 are for main parts, headings at Level 2 are for subsections, and so on. Headings help the reader find their way around your work and make it easier to read.

2.3 The Page Layout and Margins

To make sure everything is the same, APA style requires certain page layout and spacing settings. On all sides of the paper, you should leave a 1-inch margin. The title page, intro, main body, and references should all have text that is aligned to the left and double-spaced. References and quotes that are very long can be single-spaced.

2.4 Numbers on Pages

Page numbers are very important for correctly referencing and citing sources. APA style puts the page numbers in the top of each page, so they are aligned with the right edge. The first page is the title page, and the page numbers go on in a straight line through the rest of the text.

2.5 Fonts and typefaces

Using the same fonts throughout your paper makes it look more professional. According to APA style, you should use a font that is easy to read, like Times New Roman or Arial, and a size of 12 points. Text should also be written in a serif style so that it is easier to read.

2.6 Indentation and Space

Double-spacing is required by APA style for the whole paper, including the main body, introduction, block quotes, and references. The only page that doesn't follow this rule is the reference page, where each item is single-spaced with two spaces between them. To show that a new paragraph has begun, the first line of each paragraph should be set back 0.5 inches from the left border.

2.7 Head Running

A running head is a shorter version of the title of your paper that shows up at the top of each page. It helps you stay consistent throughout your work and gives you a quick reference. The moving head should only have 50 characters, including spaces and punctuation. It should be written in capital letters.

2.8 Charts and tables

APA style tells you how to organize tables and figures when you use them to show data or pictures in your paper. Each table or figure should have a number that goes with it and a title that describes it. Tables are used to show facts in a list format, while figures are things like graphs, charts, and pictures. They should be cited correctly and put in the main body of the work.

2.9 Citations and Sources

Citations and references should be talked about in more detail in later parts, but for now it's important to know what they mean in terms of formatting rules. APA style has rules about how to cite sources in the text and how to make a reference list. These rules make sure that sources are properly credited and make it easy for readers to find the works that were referenced.

2.10 In Brief

An abstract is a short summary of the main points and results of your work. It gives a short summary of the problem or question that was researched, the methods used, the results, and the findings. You should put the abstract on a different page after the title page. It shouldn't be longer than 250 words.

Following these formatting rules will help you show your schoolwork in a clear and consistent way that makes it easier to read and makes sure everything is the same. We will talk about the details of in-text citations and references in the next chapter. These are important for giving credit to sources and making your study seem more reliable.

3

In-Text Citations and References

This chapter builds on the layout rules we talked about in Chapter 2 by going into more detail about the most important parts of APA style in-text citations and references. In-text quotations are used to give credit to the sources of information in the main body of your work. The reference list, on the other hand, has a complete list of all the sources you used in your paper.

3.1 Citations in the Text

In-text quotations are short references to a source that you use in your writing. In APA style, they are used to give credit to the original writers and help readers find the source that was used. In-text citations give readers the information they need to find the appropriate entry in the reference list.

The last name of the author and the year of release should be enclosed in parentheses in an in-text citation. As an example (Smith, 2021). If the author's name is in the sentence, only the year of release needs to be put in parentheses. For example, Smith (2021) says that...

3.2 Straight Quotes

When you quote straight from a source, you must include the page number(s) in your in-text citation. This makes it easier for people to find the exact text you are talking about. A direct quotation reference should have the last name of the author, the year it was published, and the page number(s) where the quote is found. such as (Smith, 2021, p. 45).

It should be written in block quote style if the quote is longer than 40 words. The whole quote is underlined and set apart from the rest of the text in a block quote. There are no quotation marks around it. In this case, the page number is not needed for the in-text number.

3.3 More than one author

When you cite a source that has more than one author, you should include all of their last names in the in-text reference for the first instance. When citing the same source again, use the last name of the first author followed by "et al." For example, (Smith, Johnson, & Brown, 2021) and (Smith et al., 2021).

3.4 Rewriting and Summarizing Text

There must still be an in-text reference when paraphrasing or summarizing information from a source. Even if you change the information to fit your own style, you should still give credit to the original source. The reference should include the last name of the author and the year the work was published.

3.5 Sources Used Before

There are times when you may find a source that is mentioned in another source. We call these second-hand sources. When you cite a secondary source, you should include both the last name of the original author and the name of the author of the work you are mentioning in the text. In the reference list, you should also list the year the main source came out and write "as cited in" after the secondary source.

3.6 List of Sources

The reference list is an important part of APA style because it tells readers more about the sources you used in your paper. The reference list is at the end of your paper and has full bibliographic information for every source you used. It is organized by the last name of the author and is in alphabetical order.

There should be a hanging indent after each mention. The first line should be flush left, and each line after that should be indented. The Publication Manual of the American Psychological Association spells out the exact format for each type of source, such as books, journal papers, and websites.

We learned the basics of how to use in-text citations and make an APA-style reference list in this lesson. These citation rules not only give credit to the original writers, but they also make it easier for readers to find and check the sources you used. To keep your academic credibility and ethics, you must learn these citation and reference rules by heart. In the next chapter, we'll talk more about the exact formats for citing different kinds of sources.

4

Citation Formats for Different Source Types in APA Style

Section 3 taught us about how important it is to use in-text sources and a reference list in APA style. Now, let's look at the exact ways to cite different types of sources that are often used in academic writing. APA style tells you how to properly cite books, journal articles, websites, and other sources so that your referencing is correct and uniform.

4.1 Book

When using APA style to cite a book, you need to include the name(s) of the author(s) or editor(s), the year it was published, the title of the book in italics or underlining, the edition (if there is one), the place where it was published, and the name of the printer. This is how it usually looks:

Author's Last Name and First Initial. (Year). Name of the book. Publisher is where.

As an example:

J. R. Smith (2021). The Parts of APA Style. Press XYZ in New York, NY.

4.2 Articles in Journals

In APA style, you need to include the name(s) of the author(s), the year the article was published, the title of the article, the journal name (in italics or underlined), the volume number, the issue number (in parentheses), and the page numbers. This is how it usually looks:

Last name, first initial of the author. (Year). Title of article. Title of the journal, volume (issue), and page range.

As an example:

The year 2021 saw Johnson, S. G., and Brown, M. L. What APA Style Does to Academic Writing. The Journal of Research, 45(2), pp. 112-125.

4.3 Online sites

In APA style, you need to list the website's author(s) or organization, the date it was published or last updated, the title of the page or article, the

URL, and the date you retrieved the information if it can change. This is how it should be written:

Author's Last Name and First Initial. This is the year, month, and day. Title of the page or file. Getting it from URL

As an example:

A. Smith (2021, September 15). How to Use APA Style. Found at https://www.example.com/apa-style

4.4 More than one author

When there are two to seven writers in a source, list all of their last names and initials in the same order that they appear in the source. If a source has eight or more authors, list the names of the first six authors, then put an ellipsis after the last author's name. As an example:

Jones, J., Johnson, A., Brown, M., et al. Why working together is important in academic research.

4.5 Sources of Electronic

Electronic sources, like eBooks, online journals, and databases, should be mentioned in the same way that print sources are. Include the required publication information, like the title, author(s), year of publication, and a way to get the information (e.g., URL or DOI). Also, if it's important, include the exact file (for example, PDF, EPUB).

4.6 Other Types of Sources

APA style tells you how to cite a lot of different kinds of sources, such as government documents, conference papers, theses, dissertations, and multimedia materials like podcasts and videos. To make sure you cite sources correctly, the American Psychological Association's Publication Manual has specific examples of how to style each type of source.

It is very important to look at the APA manual or a good APA style guide for detailed directions on how to correctly cite different types of sources. When you use the right citation formats, you give credit to the original writers and make it easy for readers to find and check the sources you used for your research.

In the next chapter, we'll talk about why it's important to be honest in school and not plagiarize, with a focus on how proper citation and referencing practices help keep scholarly ethics.

5

Academic Integrity

Academic integrity is an important part of scholarly writing because it supports moral standards and makes sure that research is reliable. This chapter will go into more detail about why academic honesty is important, the different kinds of plagiarism you should be aware of, and how to avoid unintentional plagiarism while still following good writing practices.

5.1 What Academic Honesty Means

Values like honesty, responsibility, and respect for intellectual property are all part of academic ethics.

It is what solid and trustworthy study is built on. Scholars show their dedication to originality, the development of knowledge, and the proper use of sources by following the rules of academic integrity.

Respecting academic integrity means doing your own study, giving credit where credit is due for other people's ideas and work, correctly citing sources, and valuing what other scholars have to say. Not only is it the right thing to do, but it also helps keep the standards of education high.

5.2 Different Kinds of Fraud

People who plagiarize are breaking the rules of academic honesty very seriously. It is important to know the different forms and appearances of copying so that you don't do it by accident:

1. Copying without attribution: This is when someone takes sentences, paragraphs, or even whole parts from a source and copies them without giving credit. It is very important to give credit to the original author for any straight quotes or information that you use.

2. Restating information or thoughts in your own words without giving credit: This is called paraphrasing. There is still a chance that it is plagiarism if the original source is not properly recognized. If you want to escape this, always cite or include a footnote when you paraphrase someone else's work.

3. Plagiarism: This is when you use someone else's work that you have already released without giving credit. It might not seem like a big deal, but passing off old work as new is unethical in the academic world. If you don't want to plagiarize your own work, you should cite and mention it like you would any other source.

4. Patchwriting: patchwriting is when you copy and rearrange text from a source while making small changes, like switching words or rephrasing lines. It is theft to not give credit to the source, even if the original text is changed. When you use information from other sources, you should always give thanks.

5. Plagiarism by omission: This is when you use someone else's work without giving credit to them. If you take information or thoughts from a source, you need to give credit where credit is due. If you don't do this, you might plagiarize without meaning to.

6. Collusion: This is when two or more people work together on a project and then turn in similar or identical work as their own, without giving credit to the other person. To be honest in school, you should always give credit to people who helped you when you turn in work that you did together.

It is important to know about these different types of plagiarism so that you don't break the rules of academic ethics by accident. You can make sure that your work is honest and original by being aware of these forms and willingly following ethics rules.

5.3 Ways to Keep Things Honest in the Classroom

To stay honest in school and avoid plagiarism, you should be proactive about the following things as you do your study and write:

1. Make a plan for your research. In your well-thought-out research plan, you should list possible sources and decide how to use them in your work. This will help you keep your routines organized and moral from the start.

2. Take accurate and complete notes: While you're doing your study, make sure you take accurate and

complete notes. Make sure you write down all the important source information, like the author(s), release year, titles, page numbers, and URLs, so that you can properly cite your sources later.

3. Learn about different ways to cite sources: Learning how to use the citation style your school requires, like APA, MLA, or Chicago, is important. For help with properly formatting citations, look at thorough style guides and use reliable sources.

4. Credit all sources: Whenever you use an idea, fact, or straight quote from a source, give credit to the source in the text or in a footnote, and also include a reference entry in your bibliography or reference list. To give credit to the original author and keep academic integrity, it is important to correctly cite sources.

5. Be careful when you paraphrase. When you do this, make sure that your own words correctly

convey the original idea. When you paraphrase someone else's work, you should always give credit in the text or in the notes, even if the words you use are your own. This will help you avoid accidentally plagiarizing.

6. Use quotation marks for straight quotes: When you quote someone else's work directly, put the text inside quotation marks. In addition to the quotation marks, you should include an in-text reference that lists the author and the exact page number where the quote can be found in the source.

7. Read and change: Before turning in your work, make sure you've properly cited all of your sources by carefully reading it again. Look over it to see if there are any mistakes or places where credit should be given, and then make the necessary changes.

8. Get help and use tools that check for plagiarism. If you're not sure how to properly cite sources or need help, ask your teacher, the library, or the writing center. You might also want to use software or online tools that check for plagiarism to help you find any instances of plagiarism that you did not mean to do in your work.

By carefully following these tips, you can make sure that your writing is honest, original, and gives credit where credit is due for other people's ideas and work.

That being said

Academic honesty is the most important thing when it comes to doing responsible and moral study and writing. Respecting and valuing other people's intellectual efforts, giving credit through correct citations, and not plagiarizing in any way are all parts of academic integrity.

You can add to the progress of knowledge while protecting the integrity and credibility of your own work by understanding how important academic honesty is, recognizing the different forms of plagiarism, and taking steps to keep your actions honest.

In the last part, we'll talk about some more resources and tools that can help you learn APA style and make sure that your writing is correct, professional, and follows ethical standards.

6

Resources for Mastering APA Style and Enhancing Writing Skills

We will look at a number of websites and tools in this last chapter that can really help you learn APA style and improve your writing in general. The purpose of these tools is to help you learn more about APA rules, format your citations correctly, get writing tips and tricks, and improve your academic writing style.

6.1 Style guides and manuals free to use online

The official Publication Manual of the American Psychological Association is one of the best ways to learn how to use APA style. This detailed guide tells you how to organize your paper, how to cite sources, and follow other rules that are unique to APA style. The guidebook is useful for researchers and writers because it can be found both in print and online.

Besides the publication guidebook, there are many online style guides and manuals that explain how to use APA style. Websites like APA Style and Purdue Online Writing Lab (OWL) have guides, lessons, and examples that are easy for writers of all levels to use. These sources explain APA rules and give advice on how to format citations, paper structure, and reference lists properly.

6.2 Software for managing citations

These days, technology has a lot of citation management tools that can make it easier to make and organize citations. Software like EndNote, Zotero, and Mendeley let you import and organize references, make in-text citations and bibliographies in a number of styles, including APA, and work on research projects with other people.

These tools for managing citations can save you time and effort while making sure that your formatting is correct and uniform. In addition, a lot of these tools work with word processors, which makes adding sources as you write very easy.

6.3 Courses and workshops on writing

To get better at writing and learn how to use APA style correctly, you might want to take part in writing groups or classes at universities, writing centers, or professional organizations. These workshops usually cover things like how to write well for school, how to make strong arguments, how to organize research papers, and how to learn different citation styles.

Additionally, a lot of schools offer online writing guides and tools that students and researchers can use to get help with APA style and other writing styles. Some of these tools are interactive modules, videos, and self-assessment quizzes that let you practice following APA rules and make sure you understand them better.

6.4 Writing Labs and Feedback from Other Students

Writing centers, which are popular in colleges and universities, are great places to get help with improving your academic writing skills. These centers offer one-on-one sessions and workshops where trained professionals or peer tutors give students helpful comments on their writing. They can help you with specific issues linked to APA style, grammar, making your ideas clear, and the overall quality of your writing.

To improve your writing skills, you can also ask your peers for comments or form writing groups. Through sharing drafts and helpful feedback, you can see where you might be able to improve, learn from other people's writing styles, and get better at using APA style.

6.5 Style and Grammar Guides

To improve your writing skills, reading other language and style guides can be helpful once you understand APA style better. You can learn more about language rules, good writing habits, and style rules other than APA from books like "The Elements of Style" by Strunk and White or "The Chicago Manual of Style."

Getting to know these resources will help you improve your overall writing skills and build a strong foundation in grammar and style, which will eventually help you follow APA guidelines.

6.6 Online Writing Groups and Forums

When you join online writing groups and forums, you can meet other writers, share your thoughts, and get help with your writing. You can ask questions about APA style on websites like Writing Stack Exchange and ResearchGate and get answers from experts. You can also talk with other researchers and writers on these sites.

You can use the information of other people in these communities, and you can also learn new writing styles and points of view that can help you improve the way you write for school.

6.7 Continued Review and Practice

Lastly, practice and rewriting are the most important things you can do to learn APA style and improve your writing skills. Writing is a skill that gets better with practice. You will get better at academic writing if you regularly practice following APA rules correctly, get feedback on your work, and make changes to your work based on that feedback.

Try to read and fix your papers with a critical eye, paying attention to things like correct citations, sentence structure, idea clarity, and consistent formatting. By thinking about your own writing and figuring out what needs work, you can improve your academic writing style and make sure you're following APA rules more closely.

That being said

Mastering APA style and getting better at writing is an ongoing process that needs a lot of practice and use of different tools. To get better at APA style, you should use online style guides, citation management software, go to writing classes, ask other people for feedback, look into grammar and style guides, join writing communities, and practice and revise your work regularly.

By using these tools regularly, you can improve your writing, make sure you always follow APA rules, and turn in accurate, professional academic work that shows you know how to do scholarly research and follow writing conventions.

Remember that learning APA style is not an end in itself. It's a way to get your ideas across and make a contribution to the academic world. Accept that you will always be able to improve your work, and look for chances to do so even more. Have fun writing!

Overcoming Writing Challenges

This chapter will talk about some of the most common writing problems that experts and writers face. No matter if you have trouble with writer's block, organization, making your ideas clear, or proofreading, we will give you useful tips and methods to get past these problems and write great work.

7.1 Stuck on Writing

Writers block is a frustrating condition in which they lose their creativity and can't move forward with their work. It can be hard to get over. One way to get past this obstacle is to use one of the following strategies:

1. Freewriting: Start with a blank page and write nonstop for a set amount of time, not thinking about spelling, grammar, or flow. This activity helps break down brain blocks and makes it easier for ideas to flow.

Outline: Use an outline or mind map to keep your ideas in order and give yourself a direction for your work. Splitting your thoughts into smaller pieces can help you handle the job more easily and concentrate on each part.

3. Change topics or sections: If you get stuck on a certain topic or section, move on to a different part of your paper for now. This shift in focus can help relieve stress and bring up new thoughts.

4. Look for motivation. Take a break and do something that makes you feel creative, like reading, listening to music, taking a walk in the woods, or doing a hobby. Taking breaks to relax and get ideas can help you get back to writing.

7.2 Structure and Organization

Keeping your structure clear and reasonable is important if you want to get your point across to readers. Here are some ways to make your work more organized and structured:

Making an outline: Before you start writing, make a thorough outline of your paper that includes the main points and arguments for each section. This will give your paper structure and make sure that your ideas run smoothly.

2. Use headings and subheadings. Use informative headings to divide your paper into parts and

subsections. This makes it easy for people to find their way around your work and understand the main points of each part.

3. Transitions: Use transitional words and sentences to connect ideas and paragraphs in a smooth way. Using words like "however," "in contrast," or "moreover" between parts of your paper helps people see how they fit together.

#4: Use a clear topic sentence to start each paragraph. This sentence should present the main idea or argument of that paragraph. This helps your writing stay coherent and leads people through it.

7.3 Making ideas clear

Think about the following ways to make sure that your thoughts are communicated clearly and effectively:

1. Use simple wording; don't use technical or overly complicated words. Instead, try to be clear by using simple, direct wording that is easy for the people you want to understand.

2. Give background and context: When you introduce an idea, theory, or study, make sure you give enough background and context information so that readers can understand why it's important and relevant.

3. Define key terms: Make sure your readers understand any key terms or ideas they may not be familiar with. This keeps everyone on the same page and stops any misunderstandings or confusion.

4. Do not tell, show: When you can, back up your claims or points with facts, examples, or data. Giving specific examples not only helps people

understand, but they also give your work more credibility.

7.4 Proofreading and editing that works

Editing and proofreading are important parts of the writing process that make sure the work is correct and free of mistakes. For good editing, think about the following tips:

1. Take a break. After you finish writing your draft, wait a little while before you start editing. This space will help you look at your work with new eyes and a more balanced point of view.

2. Read your work out loud. Reading your work out loud can help you find awkward language, phrases that go on too long, or ideas that aren't clear. Hearing the words can bring up problems that you might not notice when reading alone.

3. Use tools to check your spelling and grammar: Use the grammar and spelling checkers that come with word editing software. Keep in mind, though, that these tools aren't perfect, so it's still important to check your work by hand.

4. Get feedback from someone outside of you. Have a friend, mentor, or coworker you trust review your work. New eyes can find mistakes or problems that you might have missed.

5. Edit in steps. Don't try to fix everything in one go; instead, focus on certain parts of your writing at a time during each edit. One pass might focus on things like spelling and language, while another might focus on things like organization and clarity.

7.5 How to Make Your Writing Strong

It takes time and practice to develop a unique and interesting writing style. Here are some tips that will help you improve the way you write:

1. Read a lot. Reading a lot in your field and other fields is one of the best ways to improve the way you write. Try out a bunch of different writing styles and methods and write down what you like.

2. Write every day. Regular writing helps you find your own style and make it stronger. Give yourself time to write every day and make it a habit to do so.

3. Try different things: Don't be afraid to try out different ways of writing, sentence patterns, or ways of making your point. Try new things; they might surprise you and help you find your own way.

4. Ask for feedback: Ask people you trust, like teachers, mentors, or peers, to give you feedback on your writing. Listen to what they have to say and use their helpful advice in the future when you write.

5. Edit and revise: The editing and revising process gives you a chance to make your writing style better. Make sure that the organization of your sentences, the words you use, and the tone you use all fit with the style and message you want to send.

That being said

Being self-aware, creative, and persistent are all things that you need to get past common writing problems. You can get past writer's block, improve organization and structure, make your ideas clearer, and create a strong writing style by doing things like freewriting, outlining, looking for inspiration, and practicing good proofreading skills.

Remember that you can always learn how to write better, and that it takes time and work to get better. Take each writing task as a chance to learn and get better, and be proud of your progress as you go. If you work hard and practice, you can become a skilled academic writer who can write work that has an effect.

8

Cultivating Effective Writing Habits

In this last part, we'll talk about how to develop good writing habits that will help you become a better and more confident writer. You can build a good writing habit that helps your long-term success by making a schedule, managing your time well, setting goals, and putting yourself first.

8.1 Making a Schedule for Writing

You need to set aside time to write every day if you want to make progress on your projects. Here are some ideas to help you get into a writing routine:

1. Figure out the best time for you to write: Find the time when you are awake, focused, and creative. Set aside your best times to write, whether they are early in the morning, late at night, or in the afternoon.

2. Set up a place to write: Make sure you have a place to write that is comfy, inspiring, and free of distractions. Get rid of any extraneous stuff and make sure you have all the tools you need.

3. Make writing goals that are attainable: For each writing session, set clear, measurable goals. You could set a goal to write a certain number of words or lines or work on revising a certain part. You can stay motivated and on track with your bigger job if you break it up into smaller, more manageable tasks.

4. Get rid of distractions: For best results, limit the things that could distract you while you're working. To do this, you might need to turn off messages on your phone or computer, disconnect from the internet, or use website blockers to stop yourself from going to sites that are distracting.

8.2 Ways to Manage Your Time

Successfully managing your time can greatly increase the amount of writing you get done. To get the most out of your writing time, think about the following tips:

1. Make writing a priority: Make writing a top goal in your daily life. Set aside time to write every day, without interruptions, and treat these times as meetings with yourself that you can't miss.

2. Use methods for blocking time: Divide your day into chunks of time that you will use for specific

tasks. Make sure you give yourself enough time for your writing projects by scheduling your writing sessions in these blocks.

3. Use techniques to get things done. Try out different techniques for getting things done, like the Pomodoro Technique, in which you work for a set amount of time (like 25 minutes) and then take a short break (like 5 minutes). This might help you stay focused and avoid getting burned out.

4. Give yourself due dates: Give yourself reasonable due dates for your writing projects and be responsible for meeting them. It can help to feel like you need to get your work done quickly and clearly if you divide it up into smaller tasks with due dates.

8.3 Setting Goals

To stay motivated and make progress with your work, you need to set goals that are clear and can be measured. Take a look at these tips for making good goals:

1. Make both long-term and short-term goals. Long-term goals give you a sense of direction and purpose, while short-term goals help you break down bigger chores into steps that you can handle. To stay motivated and keep track of your progress, find a mix between these two types of goals.

2. Set clear, measurable goals. For example, you could say what you want to achieve in terms of word count, parts finished, or specific milestones. This makes it easy to see how you're doing and gives you a sense of satisfaction when you reach your goals.

3. Write down your goals. Put your goals somewhere you can see them, like a book or a whiteboard near where you write. Review and

change your goals often to make sure they are still relevant and doable.

4. Celebrate your successes. When you hit a goal or important point, you should take some time to celebrate and appreciate your progress. Giving yourself rewards for your hard work can keep you going and make you feel good about what you've done.

8.4 Taking care of yourself and your health

Putting yourself first is important for staying motivated, mentally healthy, and productive over time. If you want to take care of your health as a writer, think about the following ideas:

1. Take breaks: Plan to take breaks from writing every so often. Do things that make you feel better, like getting up and stretching. Breaks help you concentrate and keep you from getting burned out.

2. Use stress-reduction and relaxation techniques: As part of your daily routine, do mindfulness techniques, deep breathing, or meditation. These habits can help you feel less stressed, concentrate better, and be more creative.

3. Keep a good mix between work and life: Separate the time you spend working from the time you spend on other things. Spend time on hobbies, exercise, and getting to know other people. Keeping work and personal life in balance is good for your health and keeps you from getting burned out.

4. Ask for help: Talk to other writers or join groups and clubs for writers. Finding people with similar challenges and hobbies can be very helpful for support, motivation, and encouragement.

In conclusion

To be successful as a writer in the long run, you need to develop good writing habits. You can make your writing practice productive and long-lasting by making it a habit, learning how to manage your time well, setting important goals, and putting yourself first.

Keep in mind that writing is a journey that requires you to keep improving and growing. Remember to be patient with yourself, see problems as chances to learn, and enjoy your growth as you go. The tips in this chapter, along with hard work and commitment, will help you improve your writing habits and become a confident and skilled writer.

Establishing a Writing Support Team

Writing is often something you do by yourself, but having someone to help you can make the process much better and give you comments and support. This chapter will talk about why it's important to have a writing support system and give you tips on how to find and keep these links strong.

9.1 What a Writing Support System Can Do for You

A writing support system can help writers at all stages of their jobs in many ways. Having a good support system can help you in the following ways:

1. Feedback and critique: Having a group of trusted people who can read your work and give you helpful feedback can help you improve it and find weak spots or blind spots.

2. Responsibility: You take responsibility when you tell other people about your goals and progress. People who care about you can help you stay inspired and on track with your writing projects.

Motivation and inspiration: Talking to other writers who love what you do can give you inspiration and motivation. They can help you get creative again when you're feeling stuck or unsure.

4. Networking and professional connections: The people who help you with your writing can be a way for you to meet with other writers, editors, publishers, or people who work in the same field. These connections can lead to new chances and groups working together.

9.2 Putting together a system to help you write

To build a writing support system, you need to find and keep in touch with people who can give you the help and support you need. Take a look at these strategies:

1. Join writing workshops or groups. Look for writing workshops or groups in your area or online where you can meet other writers. A lot of the time, these communities let people share their work, get comments, and meet new people.

2. Go to writing conferences or events: To meet other writers and people working in the writing business, go to writing conferences, author readings, or literary events. These chances can help you make useful links and maybe even find a mentor.

3. Use online tools: Join writing groups and forums where other writers get together to talk about their work, share resources, and help each other. Online critique boards and social media groups that focus on writing can be used as a virtual support system.

4. Look for writing friends. You can trade work and get feedback from a writing partner or critique group. Having a close writing friend can help you learn more about each other's styles and give you support and feedback all the time.

9.3 Taking Care of Your Writing Support Group

Once you've made connections with people in your writing support system, it's important to keep those ties alive. Here are some ways to build good relationships:

1. Give help and feedback. A method for writing help works both ways. Take an active role in giving your fellow writers comments and support. Honor their accomplishments and give them helpful advice when they need it.

2. Go to events that have to do with writing. Go to meetings, classes, or other writing-related events that your writing support system sets up. By doing these things on a regular basis, you will improve your relationships and become more involved in the community.

3. Share resources and opportunities: Help other writers out by giving them resources, knowledge about the industry, and writing opportunities.

Sharing and working together can build community and a sense of exchange.

4. Stay in touch with your writing support system both online and off. To do this, use online tools like social media groups or virtual meet-ups. Additionally, try to get together in person as often as possible to build stronger relationships.

9.4 Keeping a safe and healthy environment

For the health and growth of everyone in your writing support system, it's important to make and keep a healthy and supportive setting. Take a look at these strategies:

1. Create a respectful and helpful environment by encouraging honest and open conversation within the group. Make sure that criticism and comments are given in a helpful way, with the focus on the work rather than the person.

2. Be open to writers from a wide range of backgrounds, points of view, and topics. Accepting difference makes the group experience better and lets members see more writing styles and ideas.

Third, set clear limits and expectations: Figure out what your writing support system is for and what its goals are. Talk about and agree on rules for sharing work, giving feedback, and valuing each other's space and privacy.

4. Celebrate wins and important milestones: No matter how big or small, let's recognize and celebrate each other's accomplishments. This kind of positive feedback makes the environment supportive, which helps people grow and keep going.

In conclusion

Getting a lot of help with your writing can really help you grow as a writer. By looking for connections, helping others, and keeping these relationships alive, you can improve your writing, get support when things get tough, and find new possibilities.

Don't forget that a writing support system is a group of people who respect, trust, and work toward the same goals. Build relationships with other writers and do what you can to help the group grow and succeed. After doing that, you'll be connected with other people who understand and value the ups and downs of the writing path.

Best of luck as you reach out to your writing support system. May you continue to do well as a writer!